THE
PRAYER
MAP
FOR
GRADS

BARBOUR
PUBLISHING

Published by Barbour Publishing, Inc., 1810 Barbour Drive, Uhrichsville, Ohio 44683, www.barbourbooks.com

Our mission is to inspire the world with the life-changing message of the Bible.

Member of the
Evangelical Christian
Publishers Association

Printed in China.

WHAT DOES PRAYER LOOK LIKE? . . .

Get ready to more fully experience the power of prayer in your everyday life with this creative journal. . .where every colorful page will guide you to create your very own prayer map—as you write out specific thoughts, ideas, and lists—which you can follow (from start to finish!) as you talk to God. (Be sure to record the date on each one of your prayer maps so you can look back over time and see how God has continued to work in your life!)

The Prayer Map for Grads will not only encourage you to spend time talking with God about the things that matter most to you as you begin your next steps into the future. . .it will also help you build a healthy spiritual habit of continual prayer for life!

DATE:

DEAR HEAVENLY FATHER,

THANK YOU FOR. . .

MY PRAYER FOR
MY FUTURE. . .

CONCERNS I NEED TO SHARE WITH YOU. . .

 I NEED YOUR WISDOM. . .

....

....

....

....

I NEED YOUR
GUIDANCE. . .

....

....

....

....

....

....

....

....

....

PLEASE HELP ME TO. . .

....

....

....

....

....

....

AMEN.
Thank You, Father,
for hearing my prayers.

"Have I not commanded you?
Be strong and courageous. Do not be afraid;
do not be discouraged, for the Lord your
God will be with you wherever you go."
JOSHUA 1:9

DATE:

DEAR HEAVENLY FATHER,

THANK YOU FOR. . .

MY PRAYER FOR
MY FUTURE. . .

CONCERNS I NEED TO SHARE WITH YOU. . .

I NEED YOUR WISDOM. . .

....
....
....
....

I NEED YOUR GUIDANCE. . .

....
....
....
....
....
....
....
....
....
....

PLEASE HELP ME TO. . .

....
....
....
....
....
....

AMEN.
Thank You, Father,
for hearing my prayers.

"With man this is impossible,
but with God all things are possible."
MATTHEW 19:26

DATE:

DEAR HEAVENLY FATHER,

THANK YOU FOR. . .

MY PRAYER FOR
MY FUTURE. . .

CONCERNS I NEED TO SHARE WITH YOU. . .

I NEED YOUR WISDOM. . .

I NEED YOUR
GUIDANCE. . .

PLEASE HELP ME TO. . .

AMEN.
Thank You, Father,
for hearing my prayers.

"Keep this Book of the Law always on your lips;
meditate on it day and night, so that you may
be careful to do everything written in it.
Then you will be prosperous and successful."

JOSHUA 1:8

DATE:

DEAR HEAVENLY FATHER,

THANK YOU FOR. . .

MY PRAYER FOR
MY FUTURE. . .

CONCERNS I NEED TO SHARE WITH YOU. . .

I NEED YOUR WISDOM. . .

I NEED YOUR GUIDANCE. . .

PLEASE HELP ME TO. . .

AMEN.
Thank You, Father,
for hearing my prayers.

*The precepts of the LORD are right,
giving joy to the heart. The commands of the
LORD are radiant, giving light to the eyes.*
PSALM 19:8

DATE:

DEAR HEAVENLY FATHER,

....
....
....
....

THANK YOU FOR. . .

....
....
....
....
....
....

MY PRAYER FOR
MY FUTURE. . .

....
....
....
....
....
....
....
....
....

CONCERNS I NEED TO SHARE WITH YOU. . .

....
....
....
....

I NEED YOUR WISDOM. . .

....

....

....

....

I NEED YOUR GUIDANCE. . .

....

....

....

....

....

....

....

....

....

....

....

PLEASE HELP ME TO. . .

....

....

....

....

....

....

....

AMEN.
Thank You, Father,
for hearing my prayers.

*Your word is a lamp for my feet,
a light on my path.*
PSALM 119:105

DATE:

DEAR HEAVENLY FATHER,

....
....
....
....

THANK YOU FOR. . .

....
....
....
....
....
....

MY PRAYER FOR
MY FUTURE. . .

....
....
....
....
....
....
....
....

CONCERNS I NEED TO SHARE WITH YOU. . .

....
....
....
....

I NEED YOUR WISDOM. . .

I NEED YOUR
GUIDANCE. . .

PLEASE HELP ME TO. . .

AMEN.
Thank You, Father,
for hearing my prayers.

*And we know that in all things God works
for the good of those who love him, who have
been called according to his purpose.*
ROMANS 8:28

DATE:

DEAR HEAVENLY FATHER,

THANK YOU FOR. . .

MY PRAYER FOR
MY FUTURE. . .

CONCERNS I NEED TO SHARE WITH YOU. . .

I NEED YOUR WISDOM. . .

I NEED YOUR
GUIDANCE. . .

PLEASE HELP ME TO. . .

AMEN.
Thank You, Father,
for hearing my prayers.

*Whoever fears the LORD has a secure fortress,
and for their children it will be a refuge.*
PROVERBS 14:26

DATE:

DEAR HEAVENLY FATHER,

THANK YOU FOR. . .

MY PRAYER FOR
MY FUTURE. . .

CONCERNS I NEED TO SHARE WITH YOU. . .

I NEED YOUR WISDOM. . .

I NEED YOUR GUIDANCE. . .

PLEASE HELP ME TO. . .

AMEN.
Thank You, Father,
for hearing my prayers.

Then [Jesus] said to them all: "Whoever wants to be
my disciple must deny themselves and take
up their cross daily and follow me."
LUKE 9:23

DATE:

DEAR HEAVENLY FATHER,

THANK YOU FOR. . .

MY PRAYER FOR
MY FUTURE. . .

CONCERNS I NEED TO SHARE WITH YOU. . .

 **I NEED YOUR WISDOM. . .**

....

....

....

....

I NEED YOUR GUIDANCE. . .

....

....

....

....

....

....

....

....

....

PLEASE HELP ME TO. . .

....

....

....

....

....

....

....

AMEN.
Thank You, Father,
for hearing my prayers.

"For the LORD your God is the one who goes with you to fight for you against your enemies to give you victory."
DEUTERONOMY 20:4

DATE:

DEAR HEAVENLY FATHER,

....
....
....
....

THANK YOU FOR. . .

....
....
....
....
....
....

MY PRAYER FOR
MY FUTURE. . .

....
....
....
....
....
....
....
....
....

CONCERNS I NEED TO SHARE WITH YOU. . .

....
....
....
....

I NEED YOUR WISDOM. . .

I NEED YOUR GUIDANCE. . .

PLEASE HELP ME TO. . .

AMEN.
Thank You, Father,
for hearing my prayers.

*Now faith is confidence in what we hope for
and assurance about what we do not see.*
HEBREWS 11:1

DATE:

DEAR HEAVENLY FATHER,

....
....
....
....

THANK YOU FOR. . .

....
....
....
....
....
....

MY PRAYER FOR
MY FUTURE. . .

....
....
....
....
....
....
....
....
....
....

CONCERNS I NEED TO SHARE WITH YOU. . .

....
....
....

 I NEED YOUR WISDOM. . .

....

....

....

....

I NEED YOUR
GUIDANCE. . .

....

....

....

....

....

....

....

....

....

....

....

PLEASE HELP ME TO. . .

....

....

....

....

....

....

....

AMEN.
Thank You, Father,
for hearing my prayers.

*Therefore, if anyone is in Christ, the new creation
has come: The old has gone, the new is here!*
2 CORINTHIANS 5:17

DATE:

DEAR HEAVENLY FATHER,

....
....
....
....

THANK YOU FOR. . .

....
....
....
....
....
....
....

MY PRAYER FOR
MY FUTURE. . .

....
....
....
....
....
....
....
....
....

CONCERNS I NEED TO SHARE WITH YOU. . .

....
....
....
....

I NEED YOUR WISDOM. . .

....

....

....

....

I NEED YOUR GUIDANCE. . .

....

....

....

....

....

....

....

....

....

....

....

PLEASE HELP ME TO. . .

....

....

....

....

....

....

....

AMEN.
Thank You, Father,
for hearing my prayers.

"But blessed is the one who trusts in the LORD, whose confidence is in him."
JEREMIAH 17:7

DATE:

DEAR HEAVENLY FATHER,

THANK YOU FOR. . .

MY PRAYER FOR
MY FUTURE. . .

CONCERNS I NEED TO SHARE WITH YOU. . .

 I NEED YOUR WISDOM. . .

....
....
....
....

I NEED YOUR GUIDANCE. . .

....
....
....
....
....
....
....
....
....
....
....

PLEASE HELP ME TO. . .

....
....
....
....
....
....
....
....

AMEN.
Thank You, Father,
for hearing my prayers.

*Being confident of this, that he who began a good
work in you will carry it on to completion
until the day of Christ Jesus.*
PHILIPPIANS 1:6

DATE:

DEAR HEAVENLY FATHER,

THANK YOU FOR. . .

MY PRAYER FOR
MY FUTURE. . .

CONCERNS I NEED TO SHARE WITH YOU. . .

I NEED YOUR WISDOM. . .

I NEED YOUR GUIDANCE. . .

PLEASE HELP ME TO. . .

AMEN.
Thank You, Father,
for hearing my prayers.

The righteous choose their friends carefully.
PROVERBS 12:26

DATE:

DEAR HEAVENLY FATHER,

THANK YOU FOR. . .

MY PRAYER FOR
MY FUTURE. . .

CONCERNS I NEED TO SHARE WITH YOU. . .

I NEED YOUR WISDOM. . .

I NEED YOUR
GUIDANCE. . .

PLEASE HELP ME TO. . .

AMEN.
Thank You, Father,
for hearing my prayers.

*Accept one another, then,
just as Christ accepted you,
in order to bring praise to God.*
ROMANS 15:7

DATE:

DEAR HEAVENLY FATHER,

THANK YOU FOR. . .

MY PRAYER FOR
MY FUTURE. . .

CONCERNS I NEED TO SHARE WITH YOU. . .

I NEED YOUR WISDOM. . .

I NEED YOUR GUIDANCE. . .

PLEASE HELP ME TO. . .

AMEN.
Thank You, Father,
for hearing my prayers.

Walk with the wise and become wise,
for a companion of fools suffers harm.
PROVERBS 13:20

DATE:

DEAR HEAVENLY FATHER,

THANK YOU FOR. . .

MY PRAYER FOR
MY FUTURE. . .

CONCERNS I NEED TO SHARE WITH YOU. . .

I NEED YOUR WISDOM. . .

I NEED YOUR
GUIDANCE. . .

PLEASE HELP ME TO. . .

AMEN.
Thank You, Father,
for hearing my prayers.

*Listen, my son, to your father's instruction and
do not forsake your mother's teaching.*
PROVERBS 1:8

DATE:

DEAR HEAVENLY FATHER,

THANK YOU FOR. . .

MY PRAYER FOR
MY FUTURE. . .

CONCERNS I NEED TO SHARE WITH YOU. . .

 I NEED YOUR WISDOM. . .

I NEED YOUR
GUIDANCE. . .

PLEASE HELP ME TO. . .

AMEN.
Thank You, Father,
for hearing my prayers.

*If it is possible, as far as it depends on you,
live at peace with everyone.*
ROMANS 12:18

DATE:

DEAR HEAVENLY FATHER,

THANK YOU FOR. . .

MY PRAYER FOR MY FUTURE. . .

CONCERNS I NEED TO SHARE WITH YOU. . .

I NEED YOUR WISDOM. . .

....
....
....
....

I NEED YOUR GUIDANCE. . .

....
....
....
....
....
....
....
....
....
....
....

PLEASE HELP ME TO. . .

....
....
....
....
....
....
....

AMEN.
Thank You, Father,
for hearing my prayers.

"And when you stand praying, if you hold anything
against anyone, forgive them, so that your Father
in heaven may forgive you your sins."
MARK 11:25

DATE:

DEAR HEAVENLY FATHER,

THANK YOU FOR. . .

MY PRAYER FOR
MY FUTURE. . .

CONCERNS I NEED TO SHARE WITH YOU. . .

I NEED YOUR WISDOM. . .

....

....

....

....

I NEED YOUR GUIDANCE. . .

....

....

....

....

....

....

....

....

....

....

....

PLEASE HELP ME TO. . .

....

....

....

....

....

....

....

AMEN.
Thank You, Father,
for hearing my prayers.

*"Do not be afraid; do not be discouraged.
Go out to face them tomorrow,
and the LORD will be with you."*
2 CHRONICLES 20:17

DATE:

DEAR HEAVENLY FATHER,

THANK YOU FOR. . .

MY PRAYER FOR
MY FUTURE. . .

CONCERNS I NEED TO SHARE WITH YOU. . .

I NEED YOUR WISDOM. . .

I NEED YOUR GUIDANCE. . .

PLEASE HELP ME TO. . .

AMEN.
Thank You, Father,
for hearing my prayers.

*I will say of the LORD, "He is my refuge
and my fortress, my God, in whom I trust."*
PSALM 91:2

DATE:

DEAR HEAVENLY FATHER,

THANK YOU FOR. . .

MY PRAYER FOR
MY FUTURE. . .

CONCERNS I NEED TO SHARE WITH YOU. . .

I NEED YOUR WISDOM. . .

....

....

....

....

I NEED YOUR
GUIDANCE. . .

....

....

....

....

....

....

....

....

....

PLEASE HELP ME TO. . .

....

....

....

....

....

....

....

AMEN.
Thank You, Father,
for hearing my prayers.

If God is for us, who can be against us?
ROMANS 8:31

DATE:

DEAR HEAVENLY FATHER,

THANK YOU FOR. . .

MY PRAYER FOR
MY FUTURE. . .

CONCERNS I NEED TO SHARE WITH YOU. . .

I NEED YOUR WISDOM. . .

I NEED YOUR
GUIDANCE. . .

PLEASE HELP ME TO. . .

AMEN.
Thank You, Father,
for hearing my prayers.

The LORD is my light and my salvation—
whom shall I fear? The LORD is the stronghold
of my life—of whom shall I be afraid?
PSALM 27:1

DATE:

DEAR HEAVENLY FATHER,

THANK YOU FOR. . .

MY PRAYER FOR
MY FUTURE. . .

CONCERNS I NEED TO SHARE WITH YOU. . .

 I NEED YOUR WISDOM. . .

I NEED YOUR
GUIDANCE. . .

PLEASE HELP ME TO. . .

AMEN.
Thank You, Father,
for hearing my prayers.

*Neither angels nor demons, neither the present nor
the future, nor any powers, neither height nor depth,
nor anything else in all creation, will be able to separate
us from the love of God that is in Christ Jesus our Lord.*
ROMANS 8:38–39

DATE:

DEAR HEAVENLY FATHER,

THANK YOU FOR. . .

MY PRAYER FOR MY FUTURE. . .

CONCERNS I NEED TO SHARE WITH YOU. . .

I NEED YOUR WISDOM. . .

I NEED YOUR
GUIDANCE. . .

PLEASE HELP ME TO. . .

AMEN.
Thank You, Father,
for hearing my prayers.

*May these words of my mouth and this
meditation of my heart be pleasing in your
sight, LORD, my Rock and my Redeemer.*
PSALM 19:14

DATE:

DEAR HEAVENLY FATHER,

THANK YOU FOR. . .

MY PRAYER FOR MY FUTURE. . .

CONCERNS I NEED TO SHARE WITH YOU. . .

 I NEED YOUR WISDOM. . .

I NEED YOUR
GUIDANCE. . .

PLEASE HELP ME TO. . .

AMEN.
Thank You, Father,
for hearing my prayers.

*Always giving thanks to God the Father for everything,
in the name of our Lord Jesus Christ.*
EPHESIANS 5:20

DATE:

DEAR HEAVENLY FATHER,

THANK YOU FOR. . .

MY PRAYER FOR
MY FUTURE. . .

CONCERNS I NEED TO SHARE WITH YOU. . .

 I NEED YOUR WISDOM. . .

I NEED YOUR GUIDANCE. . .

PLEASE HELP ME TO. . .

AMEN.
Thank You, Father,
for hearing my prayers.

Humility is the fear of the LORD;
its wages are riches and honor and life.
PROVERBS 22:4

DATE:

DEAR HEAVENLY FATHER,

....

....

....

....

THANK YOU FOR. . .

....

....

....

....

....

....

....

MY PRAYER FOR
MY FUTURE. . .

....

....

....

....

....

....

....

....

....

....

CONCERNS I NEED TO SHARE WITH YOU. . .

....

....

....

....

I NEED YOUR WISDOM. . .

....

....

....

....

I NEED YOUR
GUIDANCE. . .

....

....

....

....

....

....

....

....

....

....

....

PLEASE HELP ME TO. . .

....

....

....

....

....

....

....

AMEN.
Thank You, Father,
for hearing my prayers.

*If we confess our sins, he is faithful and
just and will forgive us our sins and
purify us from all unrighteousness.*
1 JOHN 1:9

DATE:

DEAR HEAVENLY FATHER,

THANK YOU FOR. . .

MY PRAYER FOR
MY FUTURE. . .

CONCERNS I NEED TO SHARE WITH YOU. . .

 I NEED YOUR WISDOM. . .

....

....

....

....

I NEED YOUR
GUIDANCE. . .

....

....

....

....

....

....

....

....

....

....

....

PLEASE HELP ME TO. . .

....

....

....

....

....

....

....

AMEN.
Thank You, Father,
for hearing my prayers.

Teach me to do your will, for you are my God;
may your good Spirit lead me on level ground.
PSALM 143:10

DATE:

DEAR HEAVENLY FATHER,

THANK YOU FOR. . .

MY PRAYER FOR
MY FUTURE. . .

CONCERNS I NEED TO SHARE WITH YOU. . .

I NEED YOUR WISDOM. . .

I NEED YOUR
GUIDANCE. . .

PLEASE HELP ME TO. . .

AMEN.
Thank You, Father,
for hearing my prayers.

Do good. . .be rich in good deeds. . .
be generous and willing to share.
1 TIMOTHY 6:18

DATE:

DEAR HEAVENLY FATHER,

....
....
....
....

THANK YOU FOR. . .

....
....
....
....
....
....

MY PRAYER FOR
MY FUTURE. . .

....
....
....
....
....
....
....
....

CONCERNS I NEED TO SHARE WITH YOU. . .

....
....
....
....

I NEED YOUR WISDOM. . .

....

....

....

....

I NEED YOUR GUIDANCE. . .

....

....

....

....

....

....

....

....

....

....

PLEASE HELP ME TO. . .

....

....

....

....

....

....

....

AMEN.

Thank You, Father,
for hearing my prayers.

*The plans of the diligent lead to profit
as surely as haste leads to poverty.*

PROVERBS 21:5

DATE:

DEAR HEAVENLY FATHER,

THANK YOU FOR. . .

MY PRAYER FOR
MY FUTURE. . .

CONCERNS I NEED TO SHARE WITH YOU. . .

I NEED YOUR WISDOM. . .

I NEED YOUR GUIDANCE. . .

PLEASE HELP ME TO. . .

AMEN.
Thank You, Father,
for hearing my prayers.

Don't let anyone look down on you because you are young, but set an example for the believers in speech, in conduct, in love, in faith and in purity.

1 TIMOTHY 4:12

DATE:

DEAR HEAVENLY FATHER,

....
....
....
....

THANK YOU FOR. . .

....
....
....
....
....
....

MY PRAYER FOR
MY FUTURE. . .

....
....
....
....
....
....
....
....
....

CONCERNS I NEED TO SHARE WITH YOU. . .

....
....
....
....

I NEED YOUR WISDOM. . .

I NEED YOUR
GUIDANCE. . .

PLEASE HELP ME TO. . .

AMEN.
Thank You, Father,
for hearing my prayers.

"Peace! Be strong now; be strong."
DANIEL 10:19

DATE:

DEAR HEAVENLY FATHER,

THANK YOU FOR. . .

MY PRAYER FOR
MY FUTURE. . .

CONCERNS I NEED TO SHARE WITH YOU. . .

I NEED YOUR WISDOM. . .

....

....

....

....

I NEED YOUR
GUIDANCE. . .

....

....

....

....

....

....

....

....

....

PLEASE HELP ME TO. . .

....

....

....

....

....

....

....

AMEN.
Thank You, Father,
for hearing my prayers.

Your hands made me and formed me;
give me understanding to learn your commands.
PSALM 119:73

DATE:

DEAR HEAVENLY FATHER,

THANK YOU FOR. . .

MY PRAYER FOR
MY FUTURE. . .

CONCERNS I NEED TO SHARE WITH YOU. . .

I NEED YOUR WISDOM. . .

I NEED YOUR GUIDANCE. . .

PLEASE HELP ME TO. . .

AMEN.
Thank You, Father,
for hearing my prayers.

*Turning your ear to wisdom and
applying your heart to understanding. . .*
PROVERBS 2:2

DATE:

DEAR HEAVENLY FATHER,

....

....

....

....

THANK YOU FOR. . .

....

....

....

....

....

....

MY PRAYER FOR
MY FUTURE. . .

....

....

....

....

....

....

....

....

....

CONCERNS I NEED TO SHARE WITH YOU. . .

....

....

....

....

I NEED YOUR WISDOM. . .

....
....
....
....

I NEED YOUR
GUIDANCE. . .

....
....
....
....
....
....
....
....
....
....
....

PLEASE HELP ME TO. . .

....
....
....
....
....
....
....
....

AMEN.
Thank You, Father,
for hearing my prayers.

*For the Spirit God gave us does not make us timid,
but gives us power, love and self-discipline.*
2 TIMOTHY 1:7

DATE:

DEAR HEAVENLY FATHER,

THANK YOU FOR. . .

MY PRAYER FOR
MY FUTURE. . .

CONCERNS I NEED TO SHARE WITH YOU. . .

I NEED YOUR WISDOM. . .

I NEED YOUR
GUIDANCE. . .

PLEASE HELP ME TO. . .

AMEN.
Thank You, Father,
for hearing my prayers.

"Love the Lord your God with all your heart
and with all your soul and with all your mind."
MATTHEW 22:37

DATE:

DEAR HEAVENLY FATHER,

THANK YOU FOR. . .

MY PRAYER FOR
MY FUTURE. . .

CONCERNS I NEED TO SHARE WITH YOU. . .

I NEED YOUR WISDOM. . .

I NEED YOUR
GUIDANCE. . .

PLEASE HELP ME TO. . .

AMEN.
Thank You, Father,
for hearing my prayers.

*And God is able to bless you abundantly, so that in
all things at all times, having all that you need,
you will abound in every good work.*
2 CORINTHIANS 9:8

DATE:

DEAR HEAVENLY FATHER,

....
....
....
....

THANK YOU FOR. . .

....
....
....
....
....

MY PRAYER FOR
MY FUTURE. . .

....
....
....
....
....
....
....
....
....

CONCERNS I NEED TO SHARE WITH YOU. . .

....
....
....
....

I NEED YOUR WISDOM. . .

I NEED YOUR
GUIDANCE. . .

PLEASE HELP ME TO. . .

AMEN.
Thank You, Father,
for hearing my prayers.

Come near to God and he will come near to you.

JAMES 4:8

DATE:

DEAR HEAVENLY FATHER,

....

....

....

....

THANK YOU FOR. . .

....

....

....

....

....

....

MY PRAYER FOR MY FUTURE. . .

....

....

....

....

....

....

....

....

....

....

CONCERNS I NEED TO SHARE WITH YOU. . .

....

....

....

....

I NEED YOUR WISDOM. . .

....

....

....

....

I NEED YOUR GUIDANCE. . .

....

....

....

....

....

....

....

....

....

....

....

PLEASE HELP ME TO. . .

....

....

....

....

....

....

....

AMEN.
Thank You, Father,
for hearing my prayers.

Above all else, guard your heart,
for everything you do flows from it.
PROVERBS 4:23

DATE:

DEAR HEAVENLY FATHER,

THANK YOU FOR. . .

MY PRAYER FOR
MY FUTURE. . .

CONCERNS I NEED TO SHARE WITH YOU. . .

I NEED YOUR WISDOM. . .

....

....

....

....

I NEED YOUR GUIDANCE. . .

....

....

....

....

....

....

....

....

....

....

PLEASE HELP ME TO. . .

....

....

....

....

....

....

....

AMEN.
Thank You, Father,
for hearing my prayers.

---

*I press on toward the goal to win the prize for which
God has called me heavenward in Christ Jesus.*

PHILIPPIANS 3:14

DATE:

DEAR HEAVENLY FATHER,

....
....
....
....

THANK YOU FOR. . .

....
....
....
....
....
....

MY PRAYER FOR
MY FUTURE. . .

....
....
....
....
....
....
....
....
....

CONCERNS I NEED TO SHARE WITH YOU. . .

....
....
....
....

I NEED YOUR WISDOM. . .

....

....

....

....

I NEED YOUR GUIDANCE. . .

....

....

....

....

....

....

....

....

....

....

....

PLEASE HELP ME TO. . .

....

....

....

....

....

....

....

....

AMEN.
Thank You, Father,
for hearing my prayers.

*For through wisdom your days will be many,
and years will be added to your life.*

PROVERBS 9:11

DATE:

DEAR HEAVENLY FATHER,

....
....
....
....

THANK YOU FOR. . .

....
....
....
....
....
....

MY PRAYER FOR
MY FUTURE. . .

....
....
....
....
....
....
....
....

CONCERNS I NEED TO SHARE WITH YOU. . .

....
....
....
....

I NEED YOUR WISDOM. . .

I NEED YOUR
GUIDANCE. . .

PLEASE HELP ME TO. . .

AMEN.
Thank You, Father,
for hearing my prayers.

The LORD is good, a refuge in times of trouble.
He cares for those who trust in him.
NAHUM 1:7

DATE:

DEAR HEAVENLY FATHER,

....
....
....
....

THANK YOU FOR. . .

....
....
....
....
....
....

MY PRAYER FOR
MY FUTURE. . .

....
....
....
....
....
....
....
....

CONCERNS I NEED TO SHARE WITH YOU. . .

....
....
....

I NEED YOUR WISDOM. . .

I NEED YOUR GUIDANCE. . .

PLEASE HELP ME TO. . .

AMEN.
Thank You, Father,
for hearing my prayers.

You make known to me the path of life;
you will fill me with joy in your presence,
with eternal pleasures at your right hand.
PSALM 16:11

DATE:

DEAR HEAVENLY FATHER,

....

....

....

....

THANK YOU FOR. . .

....

....

....

....

....

....

MY PRAYER FOR
MY FUTURE. . .

....

....

....

....

....

....

....

....

....

CONCERNS I NEED TO SHARE WITH YOU. . .

....

....

....

....

I NEED YOUR WISDOM. . .

....

....

....

....

I NEED YOUR GUIDANCE. . .

....

....

....

....

....

....

....

....

....

....

PLEASE HELP ME TO. . .

....

....

....

....

....

AMEN.
Thank You, Father,
for hearing my prayers.

*Whoever heeds discipline shows the way to life,
but whoever ignores correction leads others astray.*

PROVERBS 10:17

DATE:

DEAR HEAVENLY FATHER,

THANK YOU FOR. . .

MY PRAYER FOR
MY FUTURE. . .

CONCERNS I NEED TO SHARE WITH YOU. . .

I NEED YOUR WISDOM. . .

I NEED YOUR
GUIDANCE. . .

PLEASE HELP ME TO. . .

AMEN.
Thank You, Father,
for hearing my prayers.

*No temptation has overtaken you except what is
common to mankind. And God is faithful; he will not
let you be tempted beyond what you can bear.
But when you are tempted, he will also provide
a way out so that you can endure it.*
1 CORINTHIANS 10:13

DATE:

DEAR HEAVENLY FATHER,

THANK YOU FOR. . .

MY PRAYER FOR
MY FUTURE. . .

CONCERNS I NEED TO SHARE WITH YOU. . .

I NEED YOUR WISDOM. . .

I NEED YOUR GUIDANCE. . .

PLEASE HELP ME TO. . .

AMEN.
Thank You, Father,
for hearing my prayers.

*I praise you because I am fearfully
and wonderfully made; your works
are wonderful, I know that full well.*
PSALM 139:14

DATE:

DEAR HEAVENLY FATHER,

THANK YOU FOR. . .

MY PRAYER FOR MY FUTURE. . .

CONCERNS I NEED TO SHARE WITH YOU. . .

I NEED YOUR WISDOM. . .

I NEED YOUR
GUIDANCE. . .

PLEASE HELP ME TO. . .

AMEN.
Thank You, Father,
for hearing my prayers.

*"Let your light shine before others,
that they may see your good deeds
and glorify your Father in heaven."*

MATTHEW 5:16

DATE:

DEAR HEAVENLY FATHER,

....
....
....
....

THANK YOU FOR. . .

....
....
....
....
....
....
....

MY PRAYER FOR
MY FUTURE. . .

....
....
....
....
....
....
....
....
....
....

CONCERNS I NEED TO SHARE WITH YOU. . .

....
....
....
....

I NEED YOUR WISDOM. . .

....

....

....

....

I NEED YOUR
GUIDANCE. . .

....

....

....

....

....

....

....

....

....

....

....

PLEASE HELP ME TO. . .

....

....

....

....

....

....

....

AMEN.
Thank You, Father,
for hearing my prayers.

*The prayer of a righteous
person is powerful and effective.*
JAMES 5:16

DATE:

DEAR HEAVENLY FATHER,

THANK YOU FOR. . .

MY PRAYER FOR MY FUTURE. . .

CONCERNS I NEED TO SHARE WITH YOU. . .

I NEED YOUR WISDOM. . .

I NEED YOUR
GUIDANCE. . .

PLEASE HELP ME TO. . .

AMEN.
Thank You, Father,
for hearing my prayers.

*Create in me a pure heart, O God,
and renew a steadfast spirit within me.*

PSALM 51:10

DATE:

DEAR HEAVENLY FATHER,

THANK YOU FOR. . .

MY PRAYER FOR
MY FUTURE. . .

CONCERNS I NEED TO SHARE WITH YOU. . .

I NEED YOUR WISDOM. . .

I NEED YOUR
GUIDANCE. . .

PLEASE HELP ME TO. . .

AMEN.
Thank You, Father,
for hearing my prayers.

Be kind and compassionate to one another,
forgiving each other, just as in Christ God forgave you.
EPHESIANS 4:32

DATE:

DEAR HEAVENLY FATHER,

THANK YOU FOR. . .

MY PRAYER FOR
MY FUTURE. . .

CONCERNS I NEED TO SHARE WITH YOU. . .

 I NEED YOUR WISDOM. . .

I NEED YOUR
GUIDANCE. . .

PLEASE HELP ME TO. . .

AMEN.
Thank You, Father,
for hearing my prayers.

*Teach us to number our days,
that we may gain a heart of wisdom.*
PSALM 90:12

DATE:

DEAR HEAVENLY FATHER,

....
....
....
....

THANK YOU FOR. . .

....
....
....
....
....
....

MY PRAYER FOR
MY FUTURE. . .

....
....
....
....
....
....
....
....
....

CONCERNS I NEED TO SHARE WITH YOU. . .

....
....
....
....

I NEED YOUR WISDOM. . .

....
....
....
....

I NEED YOUR
GUIDANCE. . .

....
....
....
....
....
....
....
....
....
....
....

PLEASE HELP ME TO. . .

....
....
....
....
....
....
....

AMEN.
Thank You, Father,
for hearing my prayers.

You, Lord, are forgiving and good,
abounding in love to all who call to you.
PSALM 86:5

DATE:

DEAR HEAVENLY FATHER,

THANK YOU FOR. . .

MY PRAYER FOR MY FUTURE. . .

CONCERNS I NEED TO SHARE WITH YOU. . .

 I NEED YOUR WISDOM. . .

....

....

....

....

I NEED YOUR GUIDANCE. . .

....

....

....

....

....

....

....

....

....

....

PLEASE HELP ME TO. . .

....

....

....

....

....

....

....

AMEN.
Thank You, Father,
for hearing my prayers.

Trust in the LORD with all your heart
and lean not on your own understanding.
PROVERBS 3:5

DATE:

DEAR HEAVENLY FATHER,

THANK YOU FOR. . .

MY PRAYER FOR
MY FUTURE. . .

CONCERNS I NEED TO SHARE WITH YOU. . .

I NEED YOUR WISDOM. . .

I NEED YOUR
GUIDANCE. . .

PLEASE HELP ME TO. . .

AMEN.
Thank You, Father,
for hearing my prayers.

I sought the LORD, and he answered me;
he delivered me from all my fears.
PSALM 34:4

DATE:

DEAR HEAVENLY FATHER,

THANK YOU FOR. . .

MY PRAYER FOR
MY FUTURE. . .

CONCERNS I NEED TO SHARE WITH YOU. . .

I NEED YOUR WISDOM. . .

I NEED YOUR
GUIDANCE. . .

PLEASE HELP ME TO. . .

AMEN.
Thank You, Father,
for hearing my prayers.

"Seek the LORD while he may be found;
call on him while he is near."
ISAIAH 55:6

DATE:

DEAR HEAVENLY FATHER,

THANK YOU FOR. . .

MY PRAYER FOR
MY FUTURE. . .

CONCERNS I NEED TO SHARE WITH YOU. . .

I NEED YOUR WISDOM. . .

....

....

....

....

I NEED YOUR
GUIDANCE. . .

....

....

....

....

....

....

....

....

....

....

PLEASE HELP ME TO. . .

....

....

....

....

....

....

....

AMEN.
Thank You, Father,
for hearing my prayers.

*And my God will meet all your needs according
to the riches of his glory in Christ Jesus.*
PHILIPPIANS 4:19

DATE:

DEAR HEAVENLY FATHER,

THANK YOU FOR. . .

MY PRAYER FOR
MY FUTURE. . .

CONCERNS I NEED TO SHARE WITH YOU. . .

 I NEED YOUR WISDOM. . .

I NEED YOUR
GUIDANCE. . .

PLEASE HELP ME TO. . .

AMEN.
Thank You, Father,
for hearing my prayers.

*But you, Lord, are a compassionate
and gracious God, slow to anger,
abounding in love and faithfulness.*
PSALM 86:15

DATE:

DEAR HEAVENLY FATHER,

....

....

....

....

THANK YOU FOR. . .

....

....

....

....

....

....

MY PRAYER FOR
MY FUTURE. . .

....

....

....

....

....

....

....

....

....

CONCERNS I NEED TO SHARE WITH YOU. . .

....

....

....

....

I NEED YOUR WISDOM. . .

....

....

....

....

I NEED YOUR GUIDANCE. . .

....

....

....

....

....

....

....

....

....

....

PLEASE HELP ME TO. . .

....

....

....

....

....

....

....

AMEN.
Thank You, Father,
for hearing my prayers.

*I cry to you, LORD; I say, "You are my refuge,
my portion in the land of the living."*
PSALM 142:5

DATE:

DEAR HEAVENLY FATHER,

THANK YOU FOR. . .

MY PRAYER FOR
MY FUTURE. . .

CONCERNS I NEED TO SHARE WITH YOU. . .

I NEED YOUR WISDOM. . .

....

....

....

....

I NEED YOUR
GUIDANCE. . .

....

....

....

....

....

....

....

....

....

....

....

PLEASE HELP ME TO. . .

....

....

....

....

....

....

....

AMEN.
Thank You, Father,
for hearing my prayers.

*And pray in the Spirit on all occasions with all kinds of
prayers and requests. With this in mind, be alert and
always keep on praying for all the Lord's people.*
EPHESIANS 6:18

DATE:

DEAR HEAVENLY FATHER,

THANK YOU FOR. . .

MY PRAYER FOR
MY FUTURE. . .

CONCERNS I NEED TO SHARE WITH YOU. . .

I NEED YOUR WISDOM. . .

I NEED YOUR
GUIDANCE. . .

PLEASE HELP ME TO. . .

AMEN.
Thank You, Father,
for hearing my prayers.

Praise be to the Lord, to God our Savior,
who daily bears our burdens.
PSALM 68:19

DATE:

DEAR HEAVENLY FATHER,

THANK YOU FOR. . .

MY PRAYER FOR
MY FUTURE. . .

CONCERNS I NEED TO SHARE WITH YOU. . .

I NEED YOUR WISDOM. . .

....

....

....

....

I NEED YOUR GUIDANCE. . .

....

....

....

....

....

....

....

....

....

PLEASE HELP ME TO. . .

....

....

....

....

....

....

....

AMEN.
Thank You, Father,
for hearing my prayers.

The prospect of the righteous is joy.
PROVERBS 10:28

DEAR HEAVENLY FATHER,

THANK YOU FOR. . .

MY PRAYER FOR
MY FUTURE. . .

CONCERNS I NEED TO SHARE WITH YOU. . .

I NEED YOUR WISDOM. . .

....

....

....

....

I NEED YOUR GUIDANCE. . .

....

....

....

....

....

....

....

....

....

....

PLEASE HELP ME TO. . .

....

....

....

....

....

....

....

AMEN.
Thank You, Father,
for hearing my prayers.

*"But blessed is the one who trusts in the LORD,
whose confidence is in him."*

JEREMIAH 17:7

DATE:

DEAR HEAVENLY FATHER,

THANK YOU FOR. . .

MY PRAYER FOR
MY FUTURE. . .

CONCERNS I NEED TO SHARE WITH YOU. . .

I NEED YOUR WISDOM. . .

I NEED YOUR
GUIDANCE. . .

PLEASE HELP ME TO. . .

AMEN.
Thank You, Father,
for hearing my prayers.

*May the God of hope fill you with all joy and peace
as you trust in him, so that you may overflow
with hope by the power of the Holy Spirit.*
ROMANS 15:13

DATE:

DEAR HEAVENLY FATHER,

THANK YOU FOR. . .

MY PRAYER FOR
MY FUTURE. . .

CONCERNS I NEED TO SHARE WITH YOU. . .

I NEED YOUR WISDOM. . .

....

....

....

....

I NEED YOUR
GUIDANCE. . .

....

....

....

....

....

....

....

....

....

....

....

PLEASE HELP ME TO. . .

....

....

....

....

....

....

AMEN.
Thank You, Father,
for hearing my prayers.

As for me, I will always have hope;
I will praise you more and more.
PSALM 71:14

DATE:

DEAR HEAVENLY FATHER,

THANK YOU FOR. . .

MY PRAYER FOR
MY FUTURE. . .

CONCERNS I NEED TO SHARE WITH YOU. . .

I NEED YOUR WISDOM. . .

....

....

....

....

I NEED YOUR GUIDANCE. . .

....

....

....

....

....

....

....

....

....

....

PLEASE HELP ME TO. . .

....

....

....

....

....

....

....

AMEN.
Thank You, Father,
for hearing my prayers.

*Let us hold unswervingly to the hope we profess,
for he who promised is faithful.*
HEBREWS 10:23

DATE:

DEAR HEAVENLY FATHER,

THANK YOU FOR. . .

MY PRAYER FOR
MY FUTURE. . .

CONCERNS I NEED TO SHARE WITH YOU. . .

I NEED YOUR WISDOM. . .

....
....
....
....

I NEED YOUR
GUIDANCE. . .

....
....
....
....
....
....
....
....
....
....
....

PLEASE HELP ME TO. . .

....
....
....
....
....
....
....

AMEN.
Thank You, Father,
for hearing my prayers.

Cause me to understand the way of your precepts,
that I may meditate on your wonderful deeds.
PSALM 119:27

DATE:

DEAR HEAVENLY FATHER,

....

....

....

....

THANK YOU FOR. . .

....

....

....

....

....

MY PRAYER FOR
MY FUTURE. . .

....

....

....

....

....

....

....

....

CONCERNS I NEED TO SHARE WITH YOU. . .

....

....

....

....

I NEED YOUR WISDOM. . .

I NEED YOUR GUIDANCE. . .

PLEASE HELP ME TO. . .

AMEN.
Thank You, Father,
for hearing my prayers.

*"All you need to say is simply 'Yes' or 'No';
anything beyond this comes from the evil one."*
MATTHEW 5:37

DATE:

DEAR HEAVENLY FATHER,

....
....
....
....

THANK YOU FOR. . .

....
....
....
....
....
....

MY PRAYER FOR
MY FUTURE. . .

....
....
....
....
....
....
....
....
....
....

CONCERNS I NEED TO SHARE WITH YOU. . .

....
....
....
....

I NEED YOUR WISDOM. . .

....

....

....

....

I NEED YOUR
GUIDANCE. . .

....

....

....

....

....

....

....

....

....

....

....

PLEASE HELP ME TO. . .

....

....

....

....

....

....

AMEN.
Thank You, Father,
for hearing my prayers.

*Whatever you have learned or received or heard
from me, or seen in me—put it into practice.
And the God of peace will be with you.*
PHILIPPIANS 4:9

DATE:

DEAR HEAVENLY FATHER,

THANK YOU FOR. . .

MY PRAYER FOR
MY FUTURE. . .

CONCERNS I NEED TO SHARE WITH YOU. . .

I NEED YOUR WISDOM. . .

....
....
....
....

I NEED YOUR
GUIDANCE. . .

....
....
....
....
....
....
....
....
....
....
....
....
....

PLEASE HELP ME TO. . .

....
....
....
....
....
....
....

AMEN.
Thank You, Father,
for hearing my prayers.

For you have been my hope, Sovereign LORD,
my confidence since my youth.
PSALM 71:5

DATE:

DEAR HEAVENLY FATHER,

THANK YOU FOR. . .

MY PRAYER FOR
MY FUTURE. . .

CONCERNS I NEED TO SHARE WITH YOU. . .

I NEED YOUR WISDOM. . .

I NEED YOUR GUIDANCE. . .

PLEASE HELP ME TO. . .

AMEN.
Thank You, Father,
for hearing my prayers.

*"Blessed rather are those
who hear the word of God and obey it."*
LUKE 11:28

DATE:

DEAR HEAVENLY FATHER,

THANK YOU FOR. . .

MY PRAYER FOR
MY FUTURE. . .

CONCERNS I NEED TO SHARE WITH YOU. . .

I NEED YOUR WISDOM. . .

....

....

....

....

I NEED YOUR
GUIDANCE. . .

....

....

....

....

....

....

....

....

....

....

....

....

PLEASE HELP ME TO. . .

....

....

....

....

....

....

....

AMEN.
Thank You, Father,
for hearing my prayers.

*And the Lord's servant must. . .
be kind to everyone, able to teach, not resentful.*
2 Timothy 2:24

DATE:

DEAR HEAVENLY FATHER,

THANK YOU FOR. . .

MY PRAYER FOR
MY FUTURE. . .

CONCERNS I NEED TO SHARE WITH YOU. . .

I NEED YOUR WISDOM. . .

I NEED YOUR
GUIDANCE. . .

PLEASE HELP ME TO. . .

AMEN.
Thank You, Father,
for hearing my prayers.

Be alert and of sober mind so that you may pray.
1 PETER 4:7

DATE:

DEAR HEAVENLY FATHER,

THANK YOU FOR. . .

MY PRAYER FOR
MY FUTURE. . .

CONCERNS I NEED TO SHARE WITH YOU. . .

I NEED YOUR WISDOM. . .

I NEED YOUR GUIDANCE. . .

PLEASE HELP ME TO. . .

AMEN.
Thank You, Father,
for hearing my prayers.

*Evildoers do not understand what is right,
but those who seek the LORD understand it fully.*

PROVERBS 28:5

DATE:

DEAR HEAVENLY FATHER,

THANK YOU FOR. . .

MY PRAYER FOR
MY FUTURE. . .

CONCERNS I NEED TO SHARE WITH YOU. . .

 I NEED YOUR WISDOM. . .

....

....

....

....

I NEED YOUR
GUIDANCE. . .

....

....

....

....

....

....

....

....

....

....

....

PLEASE HELP ME TO. . .

....

....

....

....

....

....

....

AMEN.
Thank You, Father,
for hearing my prayers.

*You will keep in perfect peace those whose minds
are steadfast, because they trust in you.*
ISAIAH 26:3

DATE:

DEAR HEAVENLY FATHER,

....
....
....
....

THANK YOU FOR. . .

....
....
....
....
....
....

MY PRAYER FOR MY FUTURE. . .

....
....
....
....
....
....
....
....
....

CONCERNS I NEED TO SHARE WITH YOU. . .

....
....
....
....

I NEED YOUR WISDOM. . .

I NEED YOUR
GUIDANCE. . .

PLEASE HELP ME TO. . .

AMEN.
Thank You, Father,
for hearing my prayers.

Many, Lᴏʀᴅ my God, are the wonders you have done,
the things you planned for us. None can compare with
you; were I to speak and tell of your deeds,
they would be too many to declare.
Psᴀʟᴍ 40:5

DATE:

DEAR HEAVENLY FATHER,

THANK YOU FOR. . .

MY PRAYER FOR
MY FUTURE. . .

CONCERNS I NEED TO SHARE WITH YOU. . .

I NEED YOUR WISDOM. . .

I NEED YOUR GUIDANCE. . .

PLEASE HELP ME TO. . .

AMEN.
Thank You, Father,
for hearing my prayers.

*As Scripture says, "Anyone who believes
in him will never be put to shame."*
ROMANS 10:11

DATE:

DEAR HEAVENLY FATHER,

THANK YOU FOR. . .

MY PRAYER FOR
MY FUTURE. . .

CONCERNS I NEED TO SHARE WITH YOU. . .

I NEED YOUR WISDOM. . .

I NEED YOUR
GUIDANCE. . .

PLEASE HELP ME TO. . .

AMEN.
Thank You, Father,
for hearing my prayers.

"Peace I leave with you; my peace I give you. I do not
give to you as the world gives. Do not let your
hearts be troubled and do not be afraid."
JOHN 14:27

DATE:

DEAR HEAVENLY FATHER,

THANK YOU FOR. . .

MY PRAYER FOR
MY FUTURE. . .

CONCERNS I NEED TO SHARE WITH YOU. . .

I NEED YOUR WISDOM. . .

I NEED YOUR
GUIDANCE. . .

PLEASE HELP ME TO. . .

AMEN.
Thank You, Father,
for hearing my prayers.

Great peace have those who love your law,
and nothing can make them stumble.
PSALM 119:165

DATE:

DEAR HEAVENLY FATHER,

THANK YOU FOR. . .

MY PRAYER FOR
MY FUTURE. . .

CONCERNS I NEED TO SHARE WITH YOU. . .

I NEED YOUR WISDOM. . .

I NEED YOUR
GUIDANCE. . .

PLEASE HELP ME TO. . .

AMEN.
Thank You, Father,
for hearing my prayers.

*Bear with each other and forgive one another if
any of you has a grievance against someone.
Forgive as the Lord forgave you.*
COLOSSIANS 3:13

DATE:

DEAR HEAVENLY FATHER,

THANK YOU FOR. . .

MY PRAYER FOR
MY FUTURE. . .

CONCERNS I NEED TO SHARE WITH YOU. . .

 I NEED YOUR WISDOM. . .

I NEED YOUR
GUIDANCE. . .

PLEASE HELP ME TO. . .

AMEN.
Thank You, Father,
for hearing my prayers.

*"The eternal God is your refuge,
and underneath are the everlasting arms."*
DEUTERONOMY 33:27

DATE:

DEAR HEAVENLY FATHER,

THANK YOU FOR. . .

MY PRAYER FOR
MY FUTURE. . .

CONCERNS I NEED TO SHARE WITH YOU. . .

I NEED YOUR WISDOM. . .

....

....

....

....

I NEED YOUR GUIDANCE. . .

....

....

....

....

....

....

....

....

....

....

....

PLEASE HELP ME TO. . .

....

....

....

....

....

....

....

AMEN.
Thank You, Father,
for hearing my prayers.

*Whatever your hand finds to do,
do it with all your might.*
ECCLESIASTES 9:10

DATE:

DEAR HEAVENLY FATHER,

....
....
....
....

THANK YOU FOR. . .

....
....
....
....
....
....
....

MY PRAYER FOR
MY FUTURE. . .

....
....
....
....
....
....
....
....
....
....

CONCERNS I NEED TO SHARE WITH YOU. . .

....
....
....
....

I NEED YOUR WISDOM. . .

....

....

....

....

I NEED YOUR GUIDANCE. . .

....

....

....

....

....

....

....

....

....

....

PLEASE HELP ME TO. . .

....

....

....

....

....

....

....

AMEN.
Thank You, Father,
for hearing my prayers.

"Ask and it will be given to you; seek and you will find; knock and the door will be opened to you. For everyone who asks receives; the one who seeks finds; and to the one who knocks, the door will be opened."

MATTHEW 7:7–8

DATE:

DEAR HEAVENLY FATHER,

THANK YOU FOR. . .

MY PRAYER FOR
MY FUTURE. . .

CONCERNS I NEED TO SHARE WITH YOU. . .

 I NEED YOUR WISDOM. . .

I NEED YOUR
GUIDANCE. . .

PLEASE HELP ME TO. . .

AMEN.
Thank You, Father,
for hearing my prayers.

*Answer me when I call to you,
my righteous God.*
PSALM 4:1

DATE:

DEAR HEAVENLY FATHER,

THANK YOU FOR. . .

MY PRAYER FOR
MY FUTURE. . .

CONCERNS I NEED TO SHARE WITH YOU. . .

I NEED YOUR WISDOM. . .

....
....
....
....

I NEED YOUR
GUIDANCE. . .

....
....
....
....
....
....
....
....
....
....
....

PLEASE HELP ME TO. . .

....
....
....
....
....
....
....
....

AMEN.
Thank You, Father,
for hearing my prayers.

Let us not become weary in doing good,
for at the proper time we will reap
a harvest if we do not give up.

GALATIANS 6:9

DATE:

DEAR HEAVENLY FATHER,

....
....
....
....

THANK YOU FOR. . .

....
....
....
....
....
....

MY PRAYER FOR
MY FUTURE. . .

....
....
....
....
....
....
....
....
....

CONCERNS I NEED TO SHARE WITH YOU. . .

....
....
....
....

I NEED YOUR WISDOM. . .

I NEED YOUR
GUIDANCE. . .

PLEASE HELP ME TO. . .

AMEN.
Thank You, Father,
for hearing my prayers.

Pray continually.
1 Thessalonians 5:17

THE PRAYER MAP FOR THE ENTIRE FAMILY. . .

The Prayer Map for Men
978-1-64352-438-2

The Prayer Map for Women
978-1-68322-557-7

The Prayer Map for Girls
978-1-68322-559-1

The Prayer Map for Boys
978-1-68322-558-4

The Prayer Map for Teens
978-1-68322-556-0

These purposeful prayer journals are a fun and creative way to more fully experience the power of prayer. Each page guides you to write out thoughts, ideas, and lists. . .which then creates a specific "map" for you to follow as you talk to God. Each map includes a spot to record the date so you can look back on your prayers and see how God has worked in your life. *The Prayer Map* not only will encourage you to spend time talking with God about the things that matter most, but also will help you build a healthy spiritual habit of continual prayer for life!

Spiral Bound / $7.99 each